LITTLE BIRD, SAY YOUR PRAYERS

LEANO DEBRA RANKO

This is a work of fiction. All names, characters, places, and incidents are a product of the author's imagination. Any resemblance to real events or persons, living or dead, is entirely coincidental.

Published by Akashic Books

ISBN: 978-1-63614-249-4

Printed in China
First printing

EU Authorized Representative details:
Easy Access System Europe
Mustamäe tee 50, 10621 Tallinn, Estonia
gpsr.request@easproject.com

Akashic Books
Instagram, X, Facebook: AkashicBooks
info@akashicbooks.com
www.akashicbooks.com

African Poetry Book Fund
Brown University
10 Prospect Street
Box A
Providence, RI 02912

TABLE OF CONTENTS

PREFACE

by Tjawangwa Dema

In *Little Bird, Say Your Prayers*, Motswana poet Leano Debra Ranko speaks of language and the body, and the "cloudy eye" of nationhood ("Shrike's Shadow"). She is unafraid to look at the body, the poet's first native landscape to which they return continually: its wounds, mucus, blood, movements, governance, all its comings and goings. She is training her storyteller's eye to know that there is no singular idea of a man, woman, or human being, no matter their locale. She reminds us at every turn that "Beauty / will not give / without taking" ("The Unlearning").

Being a fellow Motswana, I recognize the linguistic milieu that is so casually entangled with the ecological in Ranko's poetry: the land, acacia trees, pelts, rivers, reeds, dust, fields, fascination with water, and so on. I recognize it not because contemporary Batswana poets working in English rely on its richness, but because my sense is that they don't do so enough, though it exists in their language and worldview: that interconnectedness which informs the Setswana calendar, totems, proverbs, practices around rainmaking and celebrating harvests, and relations to the animal world. I do not mean to burden Ranko with a duty none of us can perform alone; I mean to celebrate the small but significant ecological narrative gestures I find in *Little Bird, Say Your Prayers*.

Given Ranko's range of interests—grief, masculinity, metamorphosis, tenderness juxtaposed with the unexpected—a fixation on the national would be counterproductive. What often matters to a first reading is whether a poem can stand pleasurably on its own, and whether it warrants a rereading. A poem, like a good rumor, should enthrall even when some details are unknown to the reader. These poems have legs; they are "filled with dogs and mildew / and a string of beads that belonged to someone's mother" ("Shrike's Shadow"). As Ranko shows us, even their bellies are "a mouth filled / with bone-white teeth" ("Shrike's Shadow").

These poems speak, which is what we ask of them. The rest is subjective.

We must remember that it is praise indeed to call a poem quotidian, lucid, or simple. Poetry goes on as life does, as we do: code-switching, changing registers, working to create meaning, attending to the local and unspectacular around us. As long as the poem doesn't become too dense a puzzle, it lends a bit of mystery, trusting us to engage with its interests. One imagines that Ranko's training as an industrial engineer stands her in good stead; her keen and curious eye is drawn to the connected architecture of things, and she has the means to tell us what she senses. What shape, she wonders, does warmth take? What form "the anatomy of grief" ("Closer to God")? How else to organize and integrate the most complex processes of life, than to reduce them to their "innards" ("Feathers"), to instruct us on "the act / of sufficient sorrow" ("Elegy for Obadiah"), and to bid us watch as the "sky breaks into confetti" ("Feathers")?

This is not a diasporic sense of place; if there is longing here, it exists within the prayer, within the dirge itself. Likewise, any alienation is from the old ways into the new. If there is any double identification, it is not between homeland and adopted country, but between a traditional idea of the female role and some "woman in the distant future" ("Alternate Universe in Which Everyone Cries after Sex"). I wanted to say that *Little Bird, Say Your Prayers* does not form collective memory, but rather a personal storying of looking around oneself. But how does one "story" without recollecting every lamb, every hill, every meridian-like wrinkle, "every grain / on the west bank" ("Salt")? So perhaps my disavowal of a diasporic tone crumbles usefully; perhaps the old binaries of here-versus-there no longer serve. Perhaps a poet looks inward and around them *as well as* outward and far away, in order to make sense, and to make stories, of wherever they are.

Often, to write a poem is to ask for a specific name, to say: what glimpse offers us the heart of the story? Whose story is this? To whom does this story matter? Ranko tells us that "To ask for a name / is to learn for certain what lies / beneath the mountain" ("Jonah and the Mountain"). Beneath Ranko's mountain, "ripe and defiant" ("Feathers"), is a mind grappling with night fire and rising suns, with the church and the body, with the future and the here and now. She knows a poet is not a truth teller, but rather a storyteller who joyfully offers lies with a grain of truth, and vice versa.

To lie well, one must imagine well. There is no failure of imagination here; it thrives and meets life head on:

Imagine a River

trickles out of the crown of my head
and bisects my body.
Lotus sprouts wind the tides
of my *this river,*
while tiny faceless men cling
to the parapets like barnacles, have made
a church out of me.

("Imagine a River")

These moments of evocative originality in the text are on trend with a growing genre of speculative writing on the continent. For a poet, they constitute an understanding that life is simultaneously here, as we see it, and elsewhere. Ranko leaps with enviable dexterity from the pliable thought of "braided flowers" to the hard junction of "pubic bones" ("The Unlearning"). What she smashes, she smashes with a soft tongue. *Little Bird, Say Your Prayers* is a gratifying read, staged by a voice that is both emerging and accomplished.

Here is a street
filled with dead men
tucked behind rumbling headlights and yards
cratered with the shrapnel droppings of a new breed
of bird chained to the skies. Here are new,
cruel gods, who have done what they have done,
left the city to wake as it does,
too poor for anything
beyond fever and empty hearths.

("Shrike's Shadow")

Here is a little bird, from a little place, with a big voice. A gorgeous introduction to a truly gifted poet!

PRAYER

There is always a war to be fought.
We wait our turn, tending land untouched
by ruin. Here, there is peace
or there is not. Sometimes blood,
if at all. Perhaps an enduring promise of mercy,
a river tall with reeds, lush with fish.

A beast's forelegs are bound with hide to keep it
from straying. And here, culture reckons with thought,
secrets buried in a forest verdant
with questions of silence: how and when to wield it.

Take this bag of gold coins and bury a piece
beneath your mother's bed. Swallow the rest.
I must teach you *tlala,* to be hungry for what
language has devoured. I must teach you, *go tlala*
to be full of questions.

TO THROW THE BABY OUT WITH THE BATHWATER

Nobody expects anyone to take these phrases literally.
They say it was a girl, though no one can truly be
certain. Perhaps it might have been named "Girl,"
a creature of tempest
known to wander the yard naked and muddied. My mother,
who is making her special leek soup,
says it does not matter what could have been. With each word
throws a pinch of salt into the pot as though
it will wash the wound of its rot. Her back
is turned to me and there are still so many things I do not recognize
about her. Sometimes I think her mouth would tell me
but all its teeth have been punched out.
I consider that I may not have been birthed but emerged fully grown from that mouth.
Later, she will creep into my bedroom
with a steaming pail and a threaded needle. She is wearing
hot-pink lipstick the color of azaleas in full bloom
pushes a worn leather strap between my teeth and recounts a winter morning
when snow transformed the red huts of her village to sugar-dusted beignets.
Every slate wiped clean.
Even the thin mucus once all the blood had run out,
the body's mutiny complete.

WRETCHED IRONY

"Water, water, every where,
Nor any drop to drink."
—Samuel Taylor Coleridge, "The Rime of the Ancient Mariner"

I.

The priest made it sound lovely. Draped in modest dresses,
heads turbaned and bowed, we etched our names in the sacred ledger.
Row by row, we knelt to receive benedictions
then proceeded to the church fountain where
he stood robed in starched white, fervor bordering
on manic as he raged at the gathered.
Linked by a chain of pinkies, our white blouses clung to heaving chests,
sweat blending with fabric. Beneath the morning light
skin gleamed, poised to crumble under the weight of scripture.
He hurled warm oil at our faces.

II.

When my wretched cousin bore the son of a married man, lured him
across the border, she was branded a smear on the family name.
I think of her sometimes, how she must have been brave,
so blatantly free. Once, she went herding with the farmhands,
trotting at their heels like a small hound.
They'd spent the morning sharpening sticks, smearing
them with poisoned lard.
That evening, they stewed rabbit, while she ran
the length of the yard
in their still-warm pelts.

III.

The windows are smeared with ashes.
His mother has strewn thorns on his grave,
to make it difficult for him to find his way home.
She knows there are things worse than death,
best left unhoped for—pain
which lacks principle and pays little heed to dignity.
The world has been indelicate with her,
has divined her responsible for her troubles
and so responsible also for her mending.
She has burned the bridge to stop herself
from crossing it.
Unseeing of all earthly things, she stares
at another god that has abandoned her.
A woman like that
will outlast us all.
Anointed.

SHRIKE'S SHADOW

Here is a house
filled with dogs and mildew
and a string of beads that belonged to someone's mother,
her mother, her mother, who remains
atop her bed, reposed in staunch prayer.
Her belly is a mouth filled
with bone-white teeth; vultures have picked
her insides clean, are lassoed to the timber of her empty kraal
perched on the thornbush that nests her young.
There are thistles between the knobs
of her spine in the smoke-blackened night; the mute blinking of stars
reminds us that not even a view of the sky is
free.
Outside, only the babies who know no better
cry, for breasts like toasted acorn husks.
Their mothers hope
every shadow is the threat of a rain-filled cloud,
that every mouth opens to the victory cry of a mirage turned lake.

Here is a street
filled with dead men
tucked behind rumbling headlights and yards
cratered with the shrapnel droppings of a new breed
of bird chained to the skies. Here are new,
cruel gods, who have done what they have done,
left the city to wake as it does,
too poor for anything
beyond fever and empty hearths.
Two knobby-kneed boys swing

the stringy corpse of what was once a boy
into a shallow hole. On this street
an old man has built a shelter for a blade of grass.
When the wind is quiet
all the men gather in an old church basement
sharing a bottle of piss.

Here is a country reduced
to dust and soot, a cloudy eye
casting judgment on heaven.
Staring death in the face, a woman labors
to her end beneath a stuttering streetlight. She knows
there will come a time when there have been no recorded births in years.
We will meet in the old churches and abandoned tunnels to weep,
name each other's children—who might grow to be poets,
make music and new-speak,
unspill the blood,
unspeak the angry litany of prayer,
pull the linger of death
from our teeth.

A KIND OF DROUGHT

Your mouth is empty. So is mine.
We have no teeth to grind the last kernels
from the withered stalks, these old arguments
we've threshed over yet another meager harvest.

The splintered masts of this house rattle
around us; a murder of crows has blackened the fields.
The silence, broken by pitiful bleats of lambs too weak to follow
the flock across the parched plains.

Over the coals you have blackened a few rats
and when our hands meet you tell me
the meat is tough.
What use have you for a woman
with hands that return empty from foraging?

You say that you love me, but you will not
return to me when the rains come.
You have shattered your back long past the dust of this village,
thankless nights gone to bed with nothing but cold
porridge and bitter tea,
useless longing, and the pity
of women who, unlike I, have earned the belt
of fat around their waists.

One evening you brought back an orange.
I could have cried
for its soft, wet breaking.

ALTERNATE UNIVERSE IN WHICH EVERYONE CRIES AFTER SEX

Even my father,
who I have witnessed cry exactly once—
enough to understand that beauty often sprouts
from instinct's soil
or the departure from reason.

When the boy lying next to me floods my bed
with tears, I think of him anew—
wet and green from his mother's womb.
I can't help but think that this boy must learn
to tend his spirit quietly even
when with every swallow comes an ache.

When his hand gathers the sweat of his brow
to trace tear-streaks on my face where I have shed none
for him, I know he has already forgiven me.
He thinks me a flower, wilted
but stubbornly lovely. Hard of will
but weak of will also, soft
and then brittle at the crossroads
of winter-cracked pipes.

The next day, our prayer is fat
with dissidence.
The boy is weeping yet again while I dream
there is a woman in the distant future
who wears her daughter's tears as a stole of judgment
on her bony shoulder—all shoulder-ed out. My hands

remain soft on the boy.
I think this is what it means
to be divine—devoted, yes,
but distant.

FOOD FOR THOUGHT

He gave me the seed and said,
"Earth."
Meteorite thoughts drove men to blindness.
Halos upon windswept tresses,
sun-licked skin.
"Sow."
Hands, broken skin,
sow.
Against meteorite thoughts,
and flesh, curling into itself;
a scythe.

THE UNLEARNING

I want to whisper to Peter Carl Fabergé
how I smashed all his precious eggs
with the wet tip of my tongue
because beautiful things are boring.
I know. I have been
where they warned us not to go.
Everyone is ugly here,
smiles often sharp
on mouths too full of opinions.
In the evenings, the women tend to a broth
of ash and lost things.
When night falls, we do not
hush our voices, do not
coddle the children. Beauty
will not give
without taking. Beauty
will pluck you bald, I learned
as we braided flowers
into our pubic bones, humming
a dirge, soft and sibilant, the path
is steep.

WARMTH

the underbelly
of a grotesque creature,
the enclosure
of the womb.

COUNTRY AS WATER

The ocean must wield itself out of the mouth that contains it.
The part that is sand, is a crevasse
threaded with bramble, muddied with remembrance
of a city no longer our own.
Despite the straining wisps of our scattered,
rosaried faith, the acacia woods
refuse to grow here. So, we do
not dare to call God by his name.

THE REVENANT

The boy draws his name
in the fog of his breath, on the window
overlooking the garden built around the apple tree,
and wipes it away—his first act of disappearance.
Now, he calls himself something
other than his name. Now, he is someone
who smiles with his fist and kisses
like shrapnel. His mouth tastes like rust,
his chest a rattling pillbox with each heave of breath—
the boy is boy no more.

The man now,
empties in his bed
which he shares only with his gun.
His stomach is a dried orange rind, ribs
despairing gateways against his skin.
Teeth marks pepper his blue-veined arms,
roses burst from his eyes, their petals
kissing down his cheeks. Grief
makes a shrine of his body
as the neighbors baptize their manicured lawns
with sighs of wet relief; their mourning
now at an end.

SALT

I am the type of man that visits the river often.
The algae have made a home of my neck,
the fish have made the soles of my feet a meal.
I know the place of every grain
on the west bank; I am always waiting
for the sun to rise.
My hands have grown heads
of their own, these fingers do as they please:
twist hair, pinch skin, bury themselves
in the scales of your tail, they bleed
into each one now red from our every embrace.
Lately, I am the man who smells dimly of salt.
My wife tells me that my kisses remind her
of the ocean, she too has now drunk of you,
has seen the memory of water trickle into her inner eye.
Our every communion has become a chapter
of farewell, as my lungs stutter over air.
I am the kind of man who pretends
to drown. My wife will find
salt tracks in the bedroom that used to be ours,
will awaken with her lips
cracked and robbed of moisture,
the kind of woman who visits the river often.

TEACH ME

Teach me
to see, to dream, to be
as water is
as is water

to receive, to take, to be gifted
to gift, to give—wholly—
away, and to,
and for.

Teach me
to see, to dream, to be
as water is
as is water;

within and in between
as without, apart,
in, and of myself
teach me

to hunger, to seek
to drink and fill
to make of skin, contentedness.

IMAGINE A RIVER

trickles out of the crown of my head
and bisects my body.
Lotus sprouts wind the tides
of my *this river,*
while tiny faceless men cling
to the parapets like barnacles, have made
a church out of me.
Blood turns on itself to devour
my *this body.*
In my belly button, tiny faceless men
sing spirituals, have made a church
out of me. How simple
this song from no mouth, the remedy
is the poison, now docked
to the tailbone of my *this body*—an old ache
when the river runs dry.
When I fear this life no longer
worth living, I will imagine
a woman's tender heaving, her sweat
as mist, manna fallen from heaven, wings
unfurling in secret
joy, stained
with the mud of myrrh and honey, the mud
of a father's raw, waiting hands. I will imagine
our corner of parched earth
soft, laughter trilling
across the empty sky, a ripe sun
over our last remaining days. Imagine
a river trickles out of the crown of my head, imagine

tiny faceless men frolic in its wake.
Imagine that they have made a church
out of me.

CLOSER TO GOD

They said they wanted to be closer to God.
Who among us can claim to not
afford the splendor of every rotten thing once ripe?
Restoration, to what is now ruin. So called
for air sticky with the smell of molasses,
wrinkled mangoes and men. Bearded,
in coveralls, beneath acid-washed hats, leathered faces—
men. Also, women.
In dusty doeks and always the smell of fever,
not a single face discernible
from the last. Suspended in a strange quiet,
in this forgotten apothecary of truth; faces
lined with fraying meridians
the anatomy of grief.
When they said they wanted to be closer to God,
who among us will deny
the cassocked dream beckoning them
near enough to touch. Though we ourselves had forgotten how,
we burnt the sage,
wet their brows with rose water,
turned our burdened souls eastward
to the rising sun.

JONAH AND THE MOUNTAIN

To ask for a name
is to learn for certain what lies
beneath the mountain.
Its walls are gouged, hollowed
by inescapable humanness.
Jonah asks his grandfather why
the neighbor's son did not return
with all the blank-faced boys. Asks why
for days after a murder of ravens darkened the skies
they heard no sound from the woods.
No rabbits in the brush, not a whisper
of the creek. Dawn brings
with it Jonah, cursing with a meatless mouth.
He pounds sorghum with feeble arms and considers the hills,
the flowers along the yard's border, knows
that the mountain will swallow him next.
Mama will not look at him. Her beetle-black eyes
are hardened into chipped coal,
washing him in the soot of stolen glances.
That evening, he finds a shard of it
at the bottom of his porridge, buries it
in the fire pit, and shuffles blind
into night's fathomless shroud.
He is never spoken of again, a nameless boy
who clings to life by the light
of the night's fire.

FEATHERS

Saturday night,
we're reading Dennis Cooper.
You are holding flames in your cheeks, blush so bright, a flame
untamed by shadow.
Nor by bullets. Nor by chains.
Stretching your throat to spill jazz-funk gut
across the bloodied floor, and the dirt road
winding home. The sky breaks into confetti
a million flashes of joy, *saints,* you're breathtaking
like this: lips poised over my open mouth
with a string of spit.
Call it rain, cleansing,
baptism.

Must we be reduced to the innards of prey, sidewalk stains, forgotten
like bloated dogs? If we are meant to
perish on the end of spears
with our names dug into the wood, let it
be in feathers—feathers so green, so blue, so yellow!
Let us die as bees, after we have stung.
In feather boas and mink so pink as to rattle
this old boneyard of mutiny. Let it be
found, in every stroke of eyeliner. Every layer
of concealer. Every mouth lined red. Or black.
Or slathered in Vaseline.
Ripe and defiant.

ALTERNATE FEMINISM

There is a stranger in the house.
He says feminism is a wound full of pus,
that if it had a face, he would carve it
with the knife he uses to butter his bread
cave it in with the fist wrapped around my hair
lick its tears from their perch, my nipple
crushed between the fine teeth of his loathing
and sorrow.
There is a stranger in the house.
He says, "*I am distance. A chasm of lost years.*" His eyes,
barbed wire around my ankles, the mouth
that tongueless swallowed his name
as though escape were a choice
I would make willingly. I have
taught myself desire, to savor its shape
on my lips, become unafraid of it. Would I dare
to speak to him of his longing, boneless
and underwhelming.
There is a stranger in the house.
She says feminism is a wound full of pus.
That if it had a face
she would sit on it gladly, drown it
in her womanhood.

ELEGY FOR OBADIAH

The sky is falling, soldier, and you are
headed to Israel. You thought heaven
a fool's consolation, worshipped
nothing and no one, your spirit
infinite until it wasn't.
When we return you to dirt,
every column of your father's kraal
is stood upon by a ram. Unusual
how they'd found you:
in a patch of sunlight
naked except for a mustard seed
beneath your tongue.

Later, after
some wet-lipped pastor you would have despised
has instructed us on the act
of sufficient sorrow, I think
to myself, *what a waste*,
of a man who never confined his laugh
to his mouth, who could not abide
dreaming alone.
You have likely convinced the ferryman
to let you walk along the river,
quiet, stern, and unendingly
curious.

ACKNOWLEDGMENTS

With grateful acknowledgment to the editors of the *Dime Show Review*, where "The Remnant" was first published.